BROKEN NO
MORE

BROKEN NO MORE

LIVING A LIFE OF WHOLENESS

Judy F. Mojica

His Glory Creations Publishing, LLC
www.hisglorycreationspublishing.com

Wendell, North Carolina

BROKEN NO MORE
Copyright © 2019 by Judy F. Mojica

All rights reserved. No part of this book may be reproduced in any form without permission in writing from the publisher, except in the case of brief quotations embodied in critical articles or reviews. Unauthorized reproduction of any part of this work is illegal and is punishable by law.

The author and publisher shall have neither liability nor responsibility for anyone with respect to any loss or damage caused directly or indirectly, by the information contained in this book.

ISBN: 978-1-950861-20-0

Scripture references are used with permission from Zondervan via Biblegateway.com

Printed in the United States of America

DEDICATION

To my beautiful daughter's Frazelle and Patience, you are my pride and joy, my constant beam of light. You are the definition of what it really means to give life.

I am ever so grateful to you both for being who you are as you have caused me to understand who I am as a wife, mother, daughter, and friend.
You are the epitome of God's gift to me and to the world. Your love is unconditional, defining, and that with abundance.

Unto you, I leave a life of legacy. A piece of who I am... broken no more as I am now whole.
My wish for you as you live your daily life and with every breath you take is that you continue to walk in the fullness of who you are, unapologetically displaying your most authentic self-breaking the rules for no one. Never forget and always remember...you are his masterpiece.

Finally, as I release you into this world that can be so cruel, I encourage you to be kind, love hard, and to thine own self be true and always, always...
Forgive ~

DEDICATION

In Loving Memory of My Mother:

Winsome smiles ever so dear, and chuckles bursting everywhere while teaching me everything you possible could I'd cling to the very essence of you.

Everything you did was with excellence, class and sophistication. Laced with drippings of laughter, it was your smile that made it all better. Only once did I ever hear or witness you cry, desperately so, I knew then mothers too could experience brokenness.

No matter the pain, you always wore a smile. Wisdom was your sister, but faith was your friend even until the end. Everything you touched was blessed, and people knew that you were someone they could confide in and trust.

Today I am who I am because you took the time to instill a wealth of knowledge into my life by sharing his word so that I may grasp with my hearts embrace the many truths of the unadulterated and uncompromised word.

For every day I reach back, I will reach for those treasures for the rest of my days. This is the moment I have longed for... To tell you all the wonderful things I have accomplished in my lifetime, yet there is not enough time in a day to share them all.

This is just the beginning for me Mommy. Sometimes sorely scared, often fancy-free, I can hardly breathe as I wait to see what's to become of me.

Although my eyes may swell up with tears, I will always remember how you taught me not to fear. I remember you once told me no matter what happens in life regarding the decisions I'd make, you will always love me.

Well, all of that and more has happened since then, but no worries , I am so much better for it and have decided to wipe my tears away, take a deep breath, fluff my hair, and apply this mascara, and oh not to forget my lip gloss! So, here I go out into this big ole world. Walking in the strength and tenacity, I've seen you walk in so many times in your life. It was because of you— Mommy! You believed in me... Now, I am able...to do just that ~

Mom (Hilda Grace Mitchell) and Dad (William Alexander Mitchell,) thank you both for teaching me how to love unconditionally.

ACKNOWLEDGMENTS

To My Family and Friends:

If you have ever experienced life, love, and or relationships - I know, without a doubt, you have had your share of immeasurable bouts of pain that were earth-shattering.

There were times you felt there was no way out - well, I am here to tell you...no matter what life brings you; you can do this! You are more than a conqueror, and yes, there is life after death. There is life after a broken relationship. **There is hope for you not just in the here and now**, but right now, you can experience love, joy, peace, happiness, and contentment right now!

Every day you are awakened by the hand of God - with every breath you take, you are given another chance to do it again...to do what? To give life...to live your life to the fullest. But this time, do it without hesitation, do it in the face of fear, master your craft. Just remember everything you put your hands to is the result of who you are. So, be the best at whatever it is. You are not a mistake. I encourage you to bring all your broken pieces to God and allow him to put them together again and watch as he masters his craft in creating the who and what you were meant to be...His masterpiece!

To my dear friend - D. Morrissey, from the highest of highs to my lowest of lows, to the ebbs and flows of my daily life. Never once have you turned your back and walked away. You are always there no matter what. Thank you for being who you are and for being my forever constant.

Last but not least, to my loving Auntie Minnie Stackhouse, thank you for your contribution to my very first book!

TABLE OF CONTENTS

Dedication .... *v*
Acknowledgements .... *viii*

God's Promises 1
Peace 11
Pain 19
Women 29
Men 41
Character 47
Wisdom 55
Friendships 67
Relationships 73
Pride 93
Strength 97
Change 101
Know Who You Are 117
Fear 123
Love 127

About the Author *137*
From the Heart of the Author *138*
Connect with Judy *139*

GOD'S PROMISES

Judy F. Mojica

I'M AFRAID

I'm afraid...it's okay, watch me,
that's it...just...like that, "He" said,
fear not my child.

What are you most afraid of?

_____

_____

_____

_____

_____

Sing to the Lord a new song, his praise from the ends of the earth, you who go down to the sea, and all that is in it, you islands, and all who live in them.

Isaiah 42:10
New International Version (NIV)

ENVISION

Write the vision down, make it plain,
it will surely come to pass~

Can you see it?

When journaling it is always important to put pen to paper. Where do you see yourself in the next three to five years?

_____
_____
_____
_____
_____
_____
_____
_____

For the vision is yet for an appointed time, but at the end, it shall speak, and not lie: though it tarry, wait for it; because it will surely come, it will not tarry.

Habakkuk 2:3
King James Version (KJV)

Waiting for someone to heal your pain is like waiting for a train that will never Come again, allow God...

When blocking out the past, we all do quite well- It is when facing one's future...is the hard part.

Name three things you feel are blocking your future success:
1. _____
_____
_____
_____

2. _____
_____
_____
_____

3. _____
_____
_____

Throwing caution to the wind is freeing and takes courage, to refrain from such takes discipline ~ Know your Boundaries!

*Have you experienced a time in which
you had to use courage?*

_____

_____

_____

_____

_____

_____

_____

The sun, sea and sand between my toes…
Just a reminder of how much you love me!

Ah, Lord God! Behold, thou hast made the heaven and the earth by thy great power and stretched out arm, and there is nothing too hard for thee:

Jeremiah 32:17
King James Version (KJV)

Judy F. Mojica

HIS PROMISES ARE FOREVER TRUE

I know He cares for me because He promised to never leave me. I know He will protect me because He promised. He said He would. I know He understands me because He felt my pain. I know He loves me because that's just who He is. This is why I know His promises are forever true.

What promises are you standing on?

_____
_____
_____
_____
_____
_____
_____
_____
_____
_____
_____

TRUSTING IN HIM

Today I choose to rest in Him…as I lean not to my own understanding. For when I am resting in Him…I am trusting in Him.

Casting all your care upon him; for he careth for you.

1 Peter 5:7
King James Version (KJV)

Search the scriptures and find as many on trust and resting in God (list below)

_____
_____
_____
_____
_____
_____
_____

A GLIMPSE OF OUR FATHER EVERLASTING

Looking up awakens the longing
to see Him as does His return
a moment that is sure to last,
for more than a couple of minutes,
Forever He covers me.

He is my eclipse.

GOD'S TIMING

Waiting on the Lord weighs heavily on the heart of those who seek to please Him. Trust the process and know that God's Timing is not your timing. Whatever you're waiting for, it will come to pass!

Whenever you're waiting on God's best for your life, remember it never looks familiar.

Have you ever felt like you heard from God, and when things take a turn for the worse, you start to question what you've heard?

_____
_____
_____
_____
_____

Yeah...me too.

Now take a moment and think about what God is saying to you. It can be anything. Seek to gain clarity. Develop an understanding about how to hear the voice of God.

NAME THREE WAYS YOU CAN HEAR FROM GOD:

1. _____
_____
_____

2. _____
_____
_____

3. _____
_____
_____

In Times of Brokenness ~ He is our Strength

Describe the time and place in life where you felt most broken.

_____
_____
_____
_____
_____
_____
_____
_____
_____
_____
_____

And he said unto me, my grace is sufficient for thee: for my strength is made perfect in weakness. Most gladly therefore will I rather glory in my infirmities, that the power of Christ may rest upon me.

2 Corinthians 12:9
King James Version (KJV)

PEACE

MASTERPIECE

Master Peace, then Create the Masterpiece!

For we are God's masterpiece. He has created us anew in Christ Jesus, so we can do the good things he planned for us long ago.

Ephesians 2:10
New Living Translation (NLT)

MUSING

Throwing Caution to the Wind

As a young girl, I would often stand gazing out the window, wondering what more there was to life. Now, as a woman looking out to sea, I watch as the ocean washes away a lifetime of memories. Yet the waves are constant, bringing me back to the place where I can be free. Free to be me in the purest form of my authenticity.

Today I see more to life than one could ever imagine! I see a life that lends everything that's meant to be. No longer living so cautiously, that I forget what being happy really means. This is why I smile...I'm happy!

Judy F. Mojica

WHISPERS OF COMFORT

THE LORD IS MY SHEPHERD I SHALL NOT WANT

The Lord is my shepherd; I shall not want. He maketh me to lie down in green pastures: he leadeth me beside the still waters. He restoreth my soul: he leadeth me in the paths of righteousness for his name's sake.

Yea, though I walk through the valley of the shadow of death, I will fear no evil: for thou art with me; thy rod and thy staff they comfort me. Thou preparest a table before me in the presence of mine enemies: thou anointest my head with oil; my cup runneth over.

Surely goodness and mercy shall follow me all the days of my life: and I will dwell in the house of the Lord forever.

Psalm 23
King James Version (KJV)

WHEN NOTHING ELSE MATTERS

And the peace of God, which passeth all understanding, shall keep your hearts and minds through Christ Jesus.

Philippians 4:7
King James Version (KJV)

What are your greatest life concerns?

_____
_____
_____
_____
_____
_____
_____
_____
_____
_____
_____

Judy F. Mojica

TEARS OF JOY

As I lie on my

bed to rest, I am

Overwhelmed with His peace.

Flooding me ever so deeply…I am full.

And God shall wipe away all tears from their eyes; and there shall be no more death, neither sorrow, nor crying, neither shall there be any more pain: for the former things are passed away.

Revelation 21:4
King James Version (KJV)

MUSING

The pages of your life can only
be written by you

Simply... Begin Again.

Are you ready to begin again? Take a moment and think...where will you begin?

_____
_____
_____
_____
_____
_____
_____
_____

The path I have been given

is the path

only

I can lead

Trust in the Lord with all thine heart; and lean not unto thine own understanding. In all thy ways acknowledge him, and he shall direct thy paths.

Proverbs 3: 5-6
King James Version (KJV)

Pain

Judy F. Mojica

SUFFERING IN SILENCE

I remember crying...

Feeling sad and lonely

Gripped with pain

Feeling paralyzed

Desperate to dispel the hurt

That ran so deep into my veins

Suffering in silence

Coping instead of doping

I was determined to shine again

Determined to sparkle once more

In every Broken piece inside

I saw my reflection

Perfect Imperfections

I asked myself daily, "Are you okay?"

I would then answer, yes

I'm okay... All while wearing a smile

Worn like a gauze

Changing it frequently

So, no one would ever know

Now, without hesitation

I Smile

MUSING

On Saturday Afternoon

Hello,

Sitting here on my couch, as I read the words of the most intricately crafted, and well-versed woman I know. It reads as follows:

I clench **tightly, my very being** from within. Snuggled up with my feet tucked under my bum. Slowly, I continue to read each word. It took everything in me to keep my eyes focused, focused long enough to make it to the end. Not to mention keeping my eyes clear of the gentle mist that filled them. I dare not blink, for if I closed my eyes, I would miss what would come next. Therefore, holding my breath so as not to interrupt the steady flow of his words...

I am at a loss for words while trying to steady the beating of my heart. I then close my eyes and think...he sees me. He knows what I look like. He understands me... even in my perfect imperfection that I am... yes, fearfully and wonderfully made. Finally...I've finished, and out comes a labored sigh from between my lips. A sigh of pure ecstasy. I am pleased and simply want to know more...

Who's speaking in this piece???

We have all experienced or longed to have that one person to be with or have as a life partner. Who is this person to you? Is this someone you have yet to let go of? How can you move forward as you release yourself from these soul ties?

_____
_____
_____
_____
_____
_____
_____
_____

> The passion that comes from your pain ultimately becomes your purpose.

Take a moment to discover what your passion is, through the remembrance of your pain. There lies your purpose.

HOLIDAY BLUES

My days are long, and my nights are just not long enough. Just as soon as the sun peaks through my blinds, I am awakened. Awakened to face another day of grief and pain. I tell myself today is going to be a good day until I am reminded of why I am (SAD) in the first place.

Holiday Blues are real, and the world is full of people who are hurting. Suffering from the loss of a loved one, a job, a home, friendships, marriage, relationships, or family connections.

I encourage you all to reach out to those who seem not to be quite like themselves lately and say hello.

If you haven't seen or heard from someone in a while, pick up the phone, send a text message to someone to let them know they are not alone. Remember, this could one day be you.

Judy F. Mojica

MUSING

The Amazing Smile

It's amazing how in the saddest of times, one can still smile so strong never flinching no matter the pain. Is it because of His strength, or is it because one has been trained to never feel again? This is the smile that keeps the painful memories away. This is the smile that helps them through the day, a smile so amazing that even in the saddest of times, one can still smile so strong.

MUSING

My Comfort Zone

Walking out of your comfort zone into a world of the unknown. My comfort zone is where no one knows. It is a place that keeps me hidden from the cruelty of this world. It is a place that shields me from hurt, harm, and danger. It is a place I let very few people in, a place where one is no longer welcome once that level of trust has been broken. I will converse with you. I will laugh with you. I will even pray for you and wish you well. But there is yet and still that place you will never have access to again, and that is my comfort zone.

A place where I let my hair down. A place where only you can know my deepest darkest secrets. A place where you then become my comfort. A place where we laugh together, sip on a glass of wine or two. Chit chat about the things that make us most happy. I may even pick a cookie up off the floor and put it to my lips, glance away to take the first bite. Just as I know, I'll never be judged by you. This is my comfort zone.

It is only then will I become who I am truly meant to be. Comfortable in my simple yet blissful state of being. Until suddenly left alone to figure it out on my own. You promised me that you would never leave. Ah, I remember these are the words spoken by those who promised to never leave me. You can trust me. Yet these are the words spoken by those whom we thought we could trust. I had hopes, we both had dreams. Dreams of becoming, living a life free of worries that would distract us from becoming complete. Complete and whole, as we drifted apart. Broken, we became never again the same. Broken into pieces no longer whole.

These are the words spoken by those…by those who are still unknown. Not because they are faceless but those who have many faces. Which, in turn, makes it easier to face less. Especially when you turn and walk away. Yes, these are the reasons we give up on life. This is the reason we find life not worth living. Therefore, we feel so alone, reasons why…we find comfort in the zone.

FACES OF PAIN

If I may, I'd like to ask if you would take a moment out of your busy schedule. There is something I want to share with you. For starters, take a moment and imagine a child who turns into a boy, who then becomes a man. Next, I want you to take a moment to remember the time in your life when you felt the most pain in your childhood.

Now, look into the face of the boy, when you were about his age, what kind of pain did you feel? Finally, look into the face of the man. Imagine the pain you now feel as a man. Is it as haunting as what you see in this picture?

The very pain you experienced as a child is the same pain you felt as a boy, and undoubtedly, ten times the magnitude of pain that overwhelms you and hits you like a ton of bricks. Unresolved, unidentified, and unspoken pain, you now feel as a man.

Measures of pain that never seem to go away. The kind of pain you avoid, suppress, and ignore. Instead of seeking help, you go into your closet to find the most decorated mask that covers up the greatest amount of pain you feel just to get through the day.

As you open your front door, you take a deep breath, display a measure of pride, and proceed to take another shot at being everything to everyone who's counting on you. Yet, you go out into the world still a "broken" man.

As you rummage through these raw emotions of your past hurt, we are going to shift things a bit. Imagine the ages of your child/ren right now and answer these questions... Do you know where they are? Do you know how they're feeling?

Have they been a bit withdrawn lately, uninterested in normal family fun and activities? Did you answer the last question they asked you? Do you even know what his/her favorite color is? Last but not least, how many times in the last few days have you sat down to have a real conversation with your child? No! I mean, allowing them to say whatever it is on their mind..."Without" any judgment, criticism or interruption?

We must do better by our children. I beg of you do not stop here. Do something about it right now. Tomorrow may very well be too late! From my heart to yours, I look forward to hearing how you made changes in how you communicate with your child/ren.

WOMEN

A SATISFIED WOMAN

A satisfied woman makes for a content woman. Now, as I relish in the woman I am becoming, my purpose is to live the life I was created to live.

Declare and Affirm:

I am *Content*

I am _____

I am _____

I am _____

I am _____

I am _____

I am _____

I am _____

I am _____

THE HEART OF A MAN

Ladies, every struggle of a man is not a reflection of his love, care, and concern for you. There's a war going on, and the struggle is real. Pray for him and trust that God will reveal His perfect plan for his life. Even if it doesn't include you
"Be that Woman."

When he makes his presence

known even in his absence,

Now this, is Priceless!

A wise woman withers not at the hands
of a wavering man,
but rather she waits.

LOYALTY OF A WOMAN

A man knows when he has encountered a loyal woman. Once the loyalty of a woman has been tampered with, you better believe the relationship will have reached its limits and is of no return.

The sad thing about this picture is no matter how many times you look at it and try to describe it, each person will have their own interpretation, consistent with that of an abstract point of view.

But the most authentic view comes from the originator of truth. He knows the very intent of the heart of a man and the deceit that lies within- the question here is, are you willing to pay the price once revealed as the counterfeit? Most women who know who they are...will not!

A REAL MAN

A "real" man will know just how to
wipe your tears away
and put a smile on your face.

NO HURRY
NO WORRIES

Ladies remember when it comes to men,
everything that looks good on the outside is not
always good on the inside. Be selective.

CONFIDENCE

When a woman knows who she is she will never
have to compete for anything...she deserves!

The Struggle is real…

If a man EVER puts you on hold for reasons unknown; the struggle is not yours, but his alone, you are now free to move along.

He who finds a wife finds a good thing and obtains favor from the Lord.

> Proverbs 18:22
> New King James Version

It no longer becomes a struggle when you know who you are as a woman. Remember, you are not an option!

TO THE YOUNG WOMAN

There are three things I would tell a young woman:

1. Always make yourself "respectfully available." Learn all you can about the male species (Man) by understanding what a man needs and remember not all boys/men are bad.

2. Yes, it is okay to love, honor, respect and obey a man (reciprocated) and to never accept anything less from a boy or a man when she is approached.

3. Finally, start praying for the man you desire to have as your husband and be realistic.

Bonus: Never build a relationship on sex!

Judy F. Mojica

A WOMAN'S WORTH

Determined on her own and within herself, this is undoubtedly true and without rebuttal. One must agree that it takes a strong man selfless and full of love and compassion to lend a bit of himself to share in the woes of the woman he has fallen for.

It is the man who doesn't have any concept of loving unconditionally, yet, he will seek out a woman to cradle him as his mother once did. But of course, he will only show you the facade of his exterior masking the most tender parts of who he is, the boy who longs to be accepted and approved by the woman he so desperately desires, yet he hides from.

The "broken" woman, the woman who has scars, chiseled from her jagged edge, every broken piece she struggles to put them together once more.

Over and over again, as it only takes one time the very core of who she is pricked by the words and actions of the man she once loved. He was the man who said all the right things, showered her with gifts and promised to be better than any other man she had ever known.

The woman who knows her worth will accept nothing less than God's best. Are you a woman who knows her worth?

Define your Worth:

Who can find a Virtuous Woman? For her worth is far above rubies. The heart of her husband safely trusts her; So, he will have no lack of gain. She does him good and not evil all the days of her life. She seeks wool and flax, and willingly works with her hands. She is like the merchant ships, she brings her food from afar.

She also rises while it is yet night, and provides food for her household and a portion for her maidservants. She considers a field and buys it; from her profits she plants a vineyard. She girds herself with strength, and strengthens her arms. She perceives that her merchandise *is* good, and her lamp does not go out by night. She stretches out her hands to the distaff and her hand holds the spindle.

She extends her hand to the poor, yes, she reaches out her hands to the needy. She is not afraid of snow for her household, for all her household is clothed with scarlet. She makes tapestry for herself; her clothing is fine linen and purple. Her husband is known in the gates, when he sits among the elders of the land. She makes linen garments and sells them, and supplies sashes for the merchants.

Strength and honor are her clothing; she shall rejoice in time to come. She opens her mouth with wisdom, and on her tongue is the law of kindness. She watches over the ways of her household, and does not eat the bread of idleness. Her children rise up and call her blessed; her husband also, and he praises her: "Many daughters have done well, But you excel them all." Charm is deceitful and beauty is passing, but a woman who fears the Lord, she shall be praised. Give her of the fruit of her hands, and let her own works praise her in the gates.

Proverbs 31:10-31
King James Version (KJV)

Judy F. Mojica

THE MIND OF A WOMAN

Who can understand the mind of a woman? Often times accused of talking in riddles, I would say you have tapped into what it means to interpret the mind of a woman.

The very connection will cause one to understand who she is by simply loving her unconditionally. To do this, one must know what it means to love and deal with her according to knowledge.

Seek not to decipher, but to understand beyond one's capacity, reaching into the heart and soul of a woman. Ultimately, we all just want to be heard.

He's Not Just a Man... He's a Gentleman!

A man is known for his character
not just for his words.

Being the head of your household does not mean you are privy to control but to lead, nor is it a place of dictatorship. Husbands love your wife as Christ loved the church. Deal with her according to knowledge and commit daily to be the godly man she can trust.

When a woman opens her heart to a man, it will only be for the man who understands her heart.

Likewise, ye husbands, dwell with them according to knowledge, giving honour unto the wife, as unto the weaker vessel, and as being heirs together of the grace of life; that your prayers be not hindered.

I Peter 3:7
King James Version (KJV)

WHAT A WOMAN WANTS

Men, if it is ever in your power to give a woman what she wants, never hesitate to give it when She Wants It... She Needs It... Give It to Her!

Gentlemen sometimes less is more. Build with someone who sees you beyond all the fluff and grow together.

The measure of a man is determined by the keeping of his word. How do you measure up??

_____
_____
_____
_____
_____

BE IT AS IT MAY...SHE'S AN "EMOTIONAL BEING"

Men never...ever think it strange when a woman is in "her feelings" and craves your attention.

Neither consider her to be "needy" when she wants you and only you.

Caring for her in such a way speaks volumes and just a bit of a reminder... Your time is coming, and you just may "need" her in the same way if not greater.

Although very strong in nature, a woman is oftentimes referred to as the weaker vessel. You'll find this in 1 Peter 3:7. Not to be mistaken as to say a woman is incapable, but rather in keeping with the context, I believe this to be true.

It is encouraged that men ought to be willing and prepared to "provide and protect" his family without hesitation. Which, in some cases, makes it easier for a woman to submit to him. On the other hand, there are many women in society today who will fight tooth and nail declaring, "I don't need a man!" Undoubtedly so, it is a fact that men and women are inherently different, and their needs vary as one becomes more independent of the other.

Consequently, by taking the approach of submitting to one another, Ephesians 5:21-24, it becomes a lot easier to accept the authority of a man as the head. When a man assumes his position as the God-head of his household. Leading with strength, confidence and who is or one of spiritual maturity. I believe it is safe to say that this may actually cause a woman to reevaluate her stance on having not just a man but a Godly- man in her life!

THE TRUTH IS...

"If you can find all of this in a good man, then you're on to something, and yep you're going to be okay." So I encourage you to… love the one you're with!

CHARACTER

MASKED

Character masked is often revealed by the subtleties of one's deceit

A TRUE SIGN OF MATURITY

Is taking ownership of one's actions or the lack thereof. Many go through life, blaming others for being "this way."
This excuse is a "cop-out" for not standing on one's own two feet.
Why not take full responsibility for the words you speak and the Impressions you leave. Especially on the lives of those
who look up to you.
Be A Man/Woman of integrity and build character. "Be that person!"

An expression of oneself is
character shown in part.

What you see in others is not always what appears to be in "real" life. Desire to become all that you are created to be, fulfilling your greatest potential. And remember...you are enough.

Credibility comes with a price, but giving credit where credit is due, is priceless!

Judy F. Mojica

MUSING

Musing on a Sunday Evening

To "simply be" the ultimate state of being with or without permission or regard of another. Stake your claim on life and... simply be!

When Duty Calls
But You Want to Go Dancing!!!

The best thing about living your life is you are the orchestrator. Meaning you can do whatever makes you happy!

What makes you happy?

_____
_____
_____
_____
_____
_____
_____
_____
_____
_____
_____
_____
_____
_____
_____

Judy F. Mojica

MUSING

Hidden Agendas

Dishonest with hidden agendas, green with envy and socially and emotionally disconnected. These are the people who come into your life with welcoming attitudes of gratitude. Thankful for you and all that you are saying all the right things to woo you in. Coaxing the innermost parts of your mind all while making you think you are the best thing since sliced bread, smothered with the finest of churned butter.

These are the same people who have left you at the front door never to reopen again. Leaving you on the sides of the curb where they pass you by, relishing in their victories that you helped them reach. Wait...yep, here it comes...the…oh, so convenient lie that somehow seems to attach itself to the glossy and supple lips of the crafty and alluring one. The one who made you feel like he/she has your best interest at hand.

The one who just couldn't seem to get enough of you. The one who was ecstatic to see you anytime you walked through the door. Whispering sweet nothings in your ear, only to mask the subtleties of their deceit. I'm sorry, you mean...Yes, that person. The one who said, I love you. The one who said, let's get together soon. The one who said, I have been just so... busy lately. The one who said, oh stop, we're family. The one who said, "I will be your friend." The one who said, "you mean so... much to me." The one who said, "never feel like you have to go it alone... I will always be here for you." Suddenly, where are these people?

Now that my Amygdala, Hippocampus, Prefrontal Cortex, Hypothalamus, and Ventral Tegmental areas have all been tampered with and after which I have borne my soul. I have come to the conclusion that maybe I don't know what it means to be a true, loyal, and committed friend, or do I? My only request to you is that no matter the part you've played in my life, from this day forward. Please, I beg of you... refuse to never lie to me again...just walk away.

Relax ~ Create ~ Never Repeat the Same Mistake Twice!

A great man once told me "don't forget where you come from."

The higher the rise, the greater the fall-Stay humble.

Pride goes before destruction, a haughty spirit before a fall.

Proverbs 16:18
New International Version (NIV)

WAIT

Some things in life are worth waiting for, trust your process.

I waited patiently for the Lord; and he inclined unto me, and heard my cry.

Psalm 40:1
King James Version (KJV)

TRUTH

The truth about speaking "truth" is no one will ever understand it unless they've lived it themselves.

COUNTERFEITS

Remember, duplicates and copycats will never...ever be able to measure up to an original you.

I will praise thee; for I am fearfully and wonderfully made: marvelous are thy works; and that my soul knoweth right well.

Psalm 139: 14
King James Version (KJV)

MUSING

Invisible Cages

Invisible Cages that are kept hidden yet so common to man. A means of capturing and masking who we really are.

The thoughts of those who seem less visible in a world daunted with the unknown, the unspeakable, the imaginable even one's past is ever before us. Fear of the unknown, unsure of the known and haunted by that which has already been shown. Invisible Cages are kept in secret veiled and unveiled when no one is watching.

Opened when least expected. Invisible cages they lock away the hurt and pain of those who pretend to be the happiest in eye view of the world.

Once the doors are open…you will see their smile miles away. On any given day and on every corner, there is another opportunity to show that yes, I do lend a helping hand when I can. Spoken with much pride by one who feels they are on top of their game. The doors of an invisible cage swings open, you come out when you feel most confident. The doors of an invisible cage close when you feel most vulnerable.

The doors of an invisible cage are shut with lock and key when threatened by the least bit of wind. Your cage is suddenly shaken. No longer sure of yourself. You begin to question your ability to face head-on that which seems so flighty. Strength is appealing, but when there is none in your mind's eye, you are weakened. The door is just about to close... if only to make it known to those surrounding me that I am more than meets the eye, I will have accomplished it once again.

There is an illusion of who I really am. The perception of the next has been overshadowed by it with the strength and ability to conquer the world. Not knowing that I am just the opposite...not because I am weak but because I am invisible. I am caged. I have been captured by my own thoughts. I am invisible because I have made myself out to be something that I am not. I say things I don't mean; I mean things I don't say. I am captured by my own words. Hindering the very essence of who I am. I long to be her. I wish I were him. Why can't my life be like that? If I had it, I'd know exactly what to do with it...whatever you're coveting. You are in an invisible cage.

A cage that only you can free yourself from. The lock and key are in your possession! You have it. You have always had a passion for the key that unlocks the cages of your heart, your mind, and your soul. There's only one thing you must understand before trying to unlock the cages of the invisible is just that…they just don't exist. Free your mind…your will and emotions. Declare that on this day, you are no longer captive to the thought of the invisible. No longer will you allow self to be tormented by the subtle whispers of that which does not even exist.

VALIDATION

Validation comes when self-reflection begins.

The significance of knowing who you are in Christ is all the validation you need in life.

REMAIN

Always remain constant, consistent, and cognizant in every area of your life. People are counting on you to show up.

There comes a time in life that we must take responsibility for our actions. Whether good, bad or indifferent. I, therefore, charge you to remain.

OPEN DOORS

The moment you realize your life is not over, doors will begin to open. Let this be a year of expectancy!

What are you believing God for?

_____
_____
_____
_____
_____

Just a reminder: Write the vision down and make it plain.

EMOTIONAL BAGGAGE

Emotional Brokenness is as universal as is the determination to lose or gain a few pounds. Sometimes it may take a coach who believes in you enough to help walk you through, so never be afraid to reach out or to seek help.

MUSING

Monday Muse

Lying to oneself is a form of self-defamation. Embellished truths are simply lies!

What's your truth?

_____
_____
_____
_____
_____
_____
_____
_____
_____
_____
_____

Monday Evening Muse

When reflecting on times past, remember to smile. It only gets better from here!

What makes you smile?

FRIENDSHIPS

Sharing in a glass of wine and making new friends is as eclectic as the next Red or White. In my opinion...the sky is blue, and I see a world of possibilities!

MAKING NEW FRIENDS

Old Friends can never be replaced, but I am so thankful for the new friends God has blessed me with!

A man that hath friends must shew himself friendly: and there is a friend that sticketh closer than a brother.

Proverbs 18: 24
King James Version (KJV)

One of the most difficult things to accomplish is genuine cohesiveness among women.

Why is it so hard for you as a woman to maintain healthy relationships with other women?

_____
_____
_____
_____
_____
_____

> All friendships aren't made to last,
> meaning some friendships are seasonal.

This is a hard lesson to learn. I couldn't understand why people (especially women) would come into my life, seemingly get what they wanted only to leave again and again. I spent years crying, sulking over why God was allowing this to happen in my life until, actually just a few years ago, I realized He was preparing me for my ultimate "call" and "purpose" in life!

I couldn't understand why I was chosen to be the one to pray these women through hard times. Hours of listening, giving words of wisdom, to praying them through. Watching these same women repeat their actions or the lack thereof expecting different results! From all my experiences up until now, I knew it was time I hone in on the path that God had for my life. All I knew to do was to push...push through and this was when Out of Brokenness was birthed.

Now I understand! I have been in training all this time, for such a time as this and had no idea. So, ladies, I encourage you to treasure each moment and just remember each friendship relationship may not be one to last forever. Your investment will bring credibility to your call, your purpose and ultimately, your passion, whatever that may be. So be that woman, be...that friend. In the end, we all win! Oh, and by the way, I'm here for you! ;)

AFRAID TO SPEAK HIGHLY OF ANOTHER?

It is a true sign of weakness and does more harm to self than the person you refuse to celebrate.

Rejoice with them that do rejoice, and weep with them that weep.

Romans 12:15
King James Version (KJV)

TRUE FRIENDSHIP IS HARD TO COME BY

Life is so much better with friends you can confide in. Friends you can trust. Friends who will never walk away. These friendships happen when you least expect it. Never take them for granted.

MUSING

Stay Real ~ Stay Relevant Stay Grounded

Having success in life has absolutely nothing to do with luck! People walk around, saying, "You are so lucky!" "How did you do this?" "I want to know who you know" yet, having no concept of what it means to be blessed and highly favored.

When your success is totally dependent on you what "you" can do and what "you" have accomplished on "your" own, you have immediately walked out from under His covering into self-sufficiency, by ultimately denying any God-given Grace or Mercy that has propelled you into greatness.

I remember it so well while sitting in the back seat of my Mum and Dad's car, as we slowly left the small town of Goldsboro N.C. (headed off to Bible College.) I remember hearing in my heart of hearts, "don't forget where you come from." I never questioned what it meant. Taking it all in stride, I kept these words close to my heart, remaining humble in all my doings. Even to this day, I can still hear these words as if it was the first time hearing them.

I have seen, heard, and been through a lot since then, encountering many situations that would cause a saved woman to curse and lose her salvation! Enduring unfortunate events such as broken friendships, broken relationships, and a broken marriage. To stay grounded was all I could do to maintain my sanity. Experiencing these life-altering events have forced me to not lean on my own understanding, but rather to trust God in every area of my life. These are the words that have kept me from a "place of pride." I have learned that no matter who I am connected with, no matter how hard life becomes, "I will always stay real, relevant, and grounded." Never forgetting… where I come from.

RELATIONSHIPS

PARENTING

Every time you belittle the thoughts and feelings of your child, they are less likely to share their problems with you. Be aware of the words you speak over your children. Speak life into them, build them up, and never break their spirit.

Fathers, do not provoke your children, lest they become discouraged

Colossians 33:21
English Standard Version (ESV)

Parents, if what you do in public is different than what you do in private, STOP it, your children are watching!

THE END OF YEAR IS HERE!

Test anxiety happens, when trying to remember all that you've learned throughout the year. You think you have it and suddenly your mind goes blank. Parents remind your child that this is just the time

Broken No More

of year to show what you know. Combat all fear with a vote of confidence!

Remember to get proper "rest" a little something for "breakfast," and don't forget to actually tell your child how "proud" you are of him/her. Sending them off with lots of "love." My prayer is for peace and that all will "succeed."

Parents, instruct for the purpose of training a child up in the way he/she should go, and avoid the "because I said so" mentality.

Train up a child in the way he should go, and when he is old he will not depart from it.

Proverbs 22:6
New King James Version (NKJV)

Have you ever told your kids, "because I said so?" What was the outcome?

_____
_____
_____
_____
_____
_____
_____
_____

Young adults are children assuming positions of adulthood without the wisdom of responsible parents, who refuse to grow up!

When I was a child, I spake as a child, I understood as a child, I thought as a child: but when I became a man, I put away childish things.

I Corinthians 13:11
Kings James Version (KJV

When a child seeks attention beyond the norm, it is inevitable that he/she will demand an audience at some point. And you, as a parent, refuse to be present at that moment?

Every time you choose to ignore your child, the greater the disconnect becomes evident in the parent/child relationship.

MY CURRENT SITUATION

One's current situation is usually described by a man or woman in a given relationship. Typically, someone who has no idea what kind of mess they have gotten themselves into.

What is your current situation and how is it serving you today?

_____

_____

_____

_____

_____

_____

There are no "perfect" marriages or relationships for that matter. So, if anyone tells you..."we never argue" Uh yeah...they're lying. The volume may have been adjusted to "silent," but oh yeah somebody is very angry!

A man who says he must be strong at all times, never allowing you to see him at his weakest point. This is a voice of a man who is crying out from a place of brokenness within.

Even when says he doesn't need you...Ladies always be his peace!

Being in a healthy relationship with oneself comes only when one has reached a state of contentment.

I am not saying this because I am in need, for I have learned to be content whatever the circumstances. I know what it is to be in need, and I know what it is to have plenty. I have learned the secret of being content in any and every situation, whether well fed or hungry, whether living in plenty or in want. I can do all this through him who gives me strength.

Philippians 4:11-13
New International Version (NIV)

Acquaintances make associates while friendships are built making great relationships.

Children most often get the short end of the stick and the brunt of all discord in a broken relationship. Pay close attention to how you speak to your former partner/spouse. Do it for the children!

I CHOOSE YOU

This may come easy for some, yet for others, it's like chatting it up with a friend you haven't seen in a while ~ The hope of reconnecting is with great anticipation. When choosing to love someone, it isn't by chance...it's by choice. So, to believe it will all come together someday soon, even when you can't see the end in sight, this is what real faith is.

Now faith is the substance of things hoped for, the evidence of things not seen.

Hebrews 11:1
King James Version (KJV)

What are you believing God for today?

_____

_____

_____

_____

_____

_____

_____

_____

DIVERSION TACTICS

If you have ever been accused of cheating, then 99.9% of the time, your partner has already cheated or is seriously thinking about cheating.

But I say unto you, that whosoever looketh on a woman to lust after her hath committed adultery with her already in his heart.

> Matthew 5:28
> King James Version (KJV)

ONE HUNDRED PERCENT

What percentage are you bringing to the table? No matter how you look at it... 50/50, 80/20, 60/40, 70/30, it all equals 100!

Unfortunately, most will see this as being unequally yoked. I'd say it all depends on how you look at it. Here's what I mean. When you are in a partnership, from a Godly standpoint, it is a known fact that there are things one's partner may not be the best at and vice versa. Consequently, this allows each partner to contribute to the relationship in whatever capacity he or she is able.

Just like every woman who wants to know she is protected and desires to feel safe without any concern or feelings of being hurt. Which includes but is not limited to the physical but in every aspect of her life. Whether it be emotionally, socially, psychologically, physically, or financially.

What are you bringing to the table?

_____

_____

_____

_____

_____

_____

_____

_____

_____

_____

_____

DADDY WHERE ARE YOU?

The day is approaching, and it just so happens to be the day many will celebrate their father. He showed you what it meant to be a woman who deserves the love and respect of a man. You long to be held by the man who once adored you. You felt loved and protected by him until he abandoned you.

He taught you how to mow the lawn and to always respect your mother. He showed you how to be a man. To protect, provide, and remain steadfast, assuming your position as the God-head of your household. He was the man you looked up to, someone you could trust.

Then there was the man who was never there. Never kept his promises. He lied to you...he hurt you...now you walk in fear.

Take back your power to no longer walk in fear, to hate, and resent the man called "Father."

I am here to tell you; you are not alone...you can live free of all past hurts and disappointments. Reach out to someone who will/can be the father you've never had. And men, be that man who will stand in the gap for the " Fatherless."

Judy F. Mojica

MUSING

Talk to Me

When the nights are lonely, and I only want to hear your voice. This is when I pick up the phone just to send a gentle text saying, Talk? In reply, you say sure. What do you want to talk about, I say, nothing? It is with the greatest understanding that he picks up the phone and dials the number that is etched in his memory.

This is the man who is so familiar with who I am that a simple hello is all that's needed to unlock the window of passion. He is the one who awakens the passion that lies within. Sighing as I remember.... memories.

THE ACT OF MARRIAGE

Is it not merely a coming together playing house or trying it out for a while to see if you like it or not? Marriage is a lifetime commitment between two people. It is a sacred union reserved for those who are deemed "ready." Saying you're ready for marriage does not constitute readiness for marriage.

For this reason, a man shall leave his father and mother and be joined to his wife, and the two shall become one flesh.

Matthew 19:5
New American Standard Bible (NASB)

ABSENCE OF THE HEART

Absence makes the heart grow fonder or...
A heart go wander!

Judy F. Mojica

Have you ever experienced an LDR (Long Distance Relationship)? If so, what were some of the challenges? Would you ever do it again?

BUILDING UP YOUR MAN

The moment a woman steps out of her rightful place as a Helpmeet for her husband, she is out of order. According to God, "It is A Good Thing When a Man Finds a Wife (Proverbs 18:22) and Obtains Favor from the Lord."

How Do I Build Up My Man?

1. Revere Him

2. Encourage Him

3. Satisfy Him

4. Pray for Him

5. Cover Him

6. Thank Him

7. Make Him Proud to Say…She's Mine!

WHAT DOES IT MEAN TO "NEED" SOMEONE?

The term "need" is and can be so misconstrued when it comes to relationships. I believe to be wanted or needed by someone is a sure sign of the humanness of mankind.

When a man or woman says, "I don't need you," it is evident that he/she is undoubtedly and indeed in need of a measure of strength that would otherwise be solidified by a loving partner. Unfortunately, because of his/her Ego, one may never admit it. Hence the reason many are single today and unfortunately will never marry.

To need someone shows great strength. It shows that one has the capacity to extend beyond the mentality of doing it alone. No man is an island or woman for that matter. Perhaps there is another way of looking at the "I don't need you, but I want you" mentality. To maintain a healthy relationship, always be clear about what you require, which includes but is not limited to your needs as well as your wants.

What are your needs?

_____
_____
_____
_____
_____
_____
_____
_____
_____
_____
_____
_____

COMPROMISE

Conflicting opinions should never be a reason to give up when "compromise" is readily available.

If it be possible, as much as lieth in you, live peaceably with all men.

Romans 12:18
King James Version (KJV)

MUSING

Broken Communication

When communicating with your spouse or significant other, it is a potential trigger point. Trigger points that may cause you or your partner to avoid or take flight. These trigger points may take on another light in the face of reality.

Meaning the things that once caused you or your partner to respond negatively may not come across as intense as in previous times. On the other hand, what was once a small trigger suddenly becomes one that causes reactions that can expose hidden wounds, which in turn can sometimes break the security or trust into pieces. Therefore, understanding who your partner is and what makes him or her tick can be a defining moment in your relationship as a couple.

Once you are aware of the trigger points of your partner, this will enable you to discern the most appropriate time in which to approach a specific concern. It is also important to take careful note in your approach as you address recurring issues to ensure better communication.

Conversely, does this mean it is "only" his responsibility to provide these things necessary to a healthy relationship? Absolutely not...every couple should set relationship goals with the understanding that to have a successful relationship, each partner must contribute no matter the percentage given.

What are your trigger points?

_____
_____
_____
_____
_____

What are your relationship goals?

_____
_____
_____
_____

PRIDE

"IT'S NOT ABOUT YOU"

When you are being attacked, know that it is not about "you" but more about what lies "within" you.

EVALUATE TO ELEVATE

How often do we seek to upstage the success of another?

Are your thoughts...I can do it better?

Who does he/she think they are?

Describe the feeling/emotion(s) that comes over you when you see someone else conquer their fears and find the strength to move forward and to simply walk in their calling.

_____
_____
_____
_____
_____
_____

If you struggle in any of these areas...
Guess what? You're not ready!!!

Pride goeth before destruction, and a haughty spirit before a fall.

Proverbs 16:18
King James Version (KJV)

MUSING

Riding on the Coattails of a Heartless Man

Riding on the coattails of a heartless man can leave a woman questioning her own ability to make good decisions. When a man shows you who he is from the start, never second guess your "woman's intuition." Go with your gut and follow your instincts.

Every flag is not meant to be a flag of surrender. Unfortunately, many a flag bleeds the color red. A flag better known as "Red flags." Red Flags that keep you wiping the tears from your eyes. The flags you refuse to take heed to after being shown over and over again. Yet, you wait to see if he will change.

Surely, he'll change, you'll say. I know he didn't mean it… I'll give him one more chance. He, on the other hand, cares as much about you as the next woman. This is the moment you should take note and never let another man take you on a ride you were never meant to go on. Ladies, always remember you are worth so much more!

What are some red flags you have missed?

_____
_____
_____
_____
_____
_____
_____
_____

STRENGTH

Judy F. Mojica

DISPLAY OF IMPERFECTIONS

When you look in the mirror who and what do you see?

> I am a woman of "passion" and "strength." Just like many of you...I laugh, I cry, and experience pain yet resilient, I remain. In silence and for far too long, I did it alone.

I feel alone when...

RECOVERING THE INEVITABLE

When you set out to make a change or to simply make a difference in one's life or in the life of another. "Growth" is inevitable and is "recovered" without default.

When life happens, then what? Hence the fact that time waits for no one. We are all challenged in life. Challenged with picking up the pieces and starting over again. Throughout one's journey in life, the ability to recover all that was lost, taken or stolen, is oftentimes restored when least expected. Sometimes by the very hand that caused the pain of devastation and other times by those whom you'd least expect it.

Remembering that it was all part of the plan. This is where you come in. In order to recover the inevitable, you must allow God to put the pieces back together again. Allow Him to take what the enemy meant for bad and turn it around for your good! Your will and desire to move forward must be part of the recovery process. So, no matter how long it takes for you to get there…even if you can't see it now, never lose sight of the prize and believe it will…happen!

Hebrews 11
King James Version (KJV)

TEMPTATIONS

Find the strength within to "complete your plan of action." Love the "one" you're with and "build upon your dreams together." Make no room for the sighted "temptations" that only last for a brief moment in time.

MOVING FORWARD

What propels me to keep moving forward? It's His strength that keeps me grounded and moving toward greatness.

What is it that keeps you moving forward?

_____
_____
_____
_____
_____
_____
_____

CHANGE

CONQUERING THE FEARS OF CHANGE

The notion that everything will always stay the same is a misnomer in a world where change is inevitable. I am suddenly paralyzed by the thought of what if. Wondering if I will make it through to the next day. Gripped by fear. I close my eyes, hoping that it will all go away. I am afraid. Reminded by the voice of my Mum, "Whatever you do keep believing in God and trust him every day and everything will be okay."

MUSING

A September to Remember

While sitting here, I began to wonder what will become of all that was lost. It is now summer's end, and not much has changed. Here a little, there a little; it all seems to be a bit vague. Racing thoughts of how I can start again. This was never to be, to start my life all over again, and having no idea what I was going to do. I have this sinking feeling in the pit of my stomach that just won't seem to go away. Painful memories of the past make me wonder if this will just be another September to remember.

BLOWING KISSES

Someone Said Tomorrow's Not Promised
So Here's to You!

Spring's approaching at Winter's past.
Make More Memories…This Time Make It Last!

SEASON'S CHANGE

What season are you currently in right now?

_____
_____
_____
_____
_____
_____
_____
_____
_____
_____
_____

There is a time for everything, and a season for every activity under the heavens:

a time to be born and a time to die,

a time to plant and a time to uproot,

a time to kill and a time to heal,

a time to tear down and a time to build,

a time to weep and a time to laugh,

a time to mourn and a time to dance,

a time to scatter stones and a time to gather them,

a time to embrace and a time to refrain from embracing,

a time to search and a time to give up,

a time to keep and a time to throw away,

a time to tear and a time to mend,

a time to be silent and a time to speak,

a time to love and a time to hate,

a time for war and a time for peace.

Ecclesiastes 3:1-11
New International Version (NIV)

FLASHBACK

Having an "ah-yeah" moment on a Friday night. Where does your mind take you when you think of that Friday night? What would you have changed if anything at all?

Every encounter forms some type of outcome, whether it be the beginning of a relationship or the end of one. We as women seek to be sought after by men, but in doing so, the outcome is not always the best. Resulting in disappointments, unrealistic expectations, dead-end situations and sometimes a broken heart. Often, we are summoned to entertain what I call "The Reach Back." This is when we reach back for what we thought was a good thing! Reaching back to the familiar or what felt good at the time. Could it be that what we thought was a good thing was only there to teach us a lesson?

Describe how you felt then and how you are feeling now as you think back on the relationships you have encountered? What lessons have you learned from your experience?

_____

_____

_____

_____

_____

_____

_____

_____

_____

_____

_____

"Expect the expected until otherwise noted."

Communication is key to any relationship. Just as unrealistic expectations can become the demise of one's broken heart. As you walk through life, remember to expect the expected until otherwise noted to avoid disappointment.

What have been some of your unrealistic expectations?

_____

_____

_____

_____

_____

_____

_____

Judy F. Mojica

MUSING

The Holiday Blues...

One of the most difficult times of the year is during this holiday season. Life is different now... Maybe your marriage is broken or no longer. The love relationship you thought would last forever just ended, or maybe you've lost a loved one, and the pain is more than you could have ever imagined.

I understand...

I understand that nothing feels right. The thoughts of being alone, not sure about what the future will hold. Remembering how it used to be and wondering if you'll ever love again. It is as piercing as the tip of an icicle. Sure, you know the importance of putting up the tree with all the trimmings, and how much the kids look forward to

the sights and sounds of Christmas, but you just... can't... bring yourself to "Make it Happen." I encourage you to dig deep and know that this too, will pass. Now go…and "Make it Happen!"
Can't wait to hear from ya!

DREAMS REALLY DO...COME TRUE

Don't Stop... Never stop;
you are far too close in reaching your destiny.

Brokenness

Ends

Where Healing Begins

NO MORE TEARS

One day God will open doors for you to share your story. Relish in the flow of tears that heal and know it is all part of the healing process.

MAKE IT HAPPEN

Do what only you can do for yourself and
"Make It Happen!"

Make sure you take time to love yourself;
you are so worth it.

The one thing that keeps me going is knowing that God is in control. He is God, who knows all. He cares about every aspect of my life. Every day He gives me the courage to live out loud...
I choose to trust him!

Casting all your care upon him; for he careth for you

I Peter 5:7
King James Version (KJV)

WORRY

"If You Worry, Don't Pray
If You Pray, Don't Worry."

By: My Auntie Pastor Minnie Stackhouse

Auntie Minnie Stackhouse

She among many of my awesome Auntie's whom I love dearly. I specifically hold dear the memory of the relationship she had with my mum, who is no longer with us. The visits, the laughter, the late-night talks on a summer's eve and how she made me feel on the day of my mother's funeral. The day was somber, and few words were spoken as I sat on the living room floor of my mum's house nestled at the feet of Aunt Minnie. I remember her saying to me, in so many words... "You can always come to my house to visit any time you want."

To this day, these words have I kept close to my heart and have realized that yes, she meant every word. It is in some of the most difficult times in life when someone reaches out to you that it means so much. Not only is her home open to me, but she has always made my daughter's Frazelle and Patience feel just as welcomed. In their words...

"Yeah, I like Aunt Minnie, and she's funny too...so, when can we visit again!"

Hence the quote. We had all just finished eating and were sitting around chatting at the end one our family reunions. Shared with such calmness, not to mention how nonchalant it came across...Aunt Minnie somehow knows how to command one's attention, simplistic at best and yet so very profound. You better believe I caught this one! Little did she know...this quote would land a spot in my first book! Yes, I was that kid, always listening for those golden nuggets of truth from my elders even as an adult.

I want to leave you all with a bit of encouragement. Never think it strange to not be accepted, respected or even celebrated by your own. But this one thing I know for sure, God will always provide for you everything you need, want, and desire when it comes to family. Take it from me...it is a hard road to travel sometimes, but never forget even when you think no one cares about you. He does and so do I.

If you desire restored relations with any of your family members, remember this quote by Stephen Covey, "Seek First to Understand, then to be Understood" 7 Habits of Highly Effective People. And finally, in the faithful words of Auntie Minnie... "If you worry, don't pray, if you pray, don't worry."

Take a moment and think about when you felt unheard. The time when you were misunderstood or when you were not given the chance to rectify the situation.

With the limited time, we have on this earth to live, make a difference, and leave a legacy. Why not take this opportunity to make it right with those who may have offended you or maybe you have offended. If I could say it in just a couple of words, it would be... Unconditional Love ~

STRESS AND ANXIETY

The stressors of life can take you down roadways of depression, anxiety, and feelings of being out of control. Take heed to the warning signs and allow time to renew your mind and rid oneself of unnecessary evils.

What in life causes you to be stressed? How do you deal with stressors?

_____

_____

_____

_____

_____

_____

_____

Do not be anxious about anything, but in every situation, by prayer and petition, with thanksgiving, present your requests to God. And the peace of God, which transcends all understanding, will guard your hearts and your minds in Christ Jesus.

Philippians 4:6-7
New International Version (NIV)

Know Who You Are

When you know who you are... the voices in your head will have to cease. When you know who you are, the world can no longer contain your peace. You are now a force to be reckoned with. When you know who you are…the world awaits you…now go out into this world so grand and assume your position and walk in your purpose!

When you "know who you are"
revenge is never an option.

It is mine to avenge; I will repay. In due time their foot will slip; their day of disaster is near and their doom rushes upon them.

Deuteronomy 32:35
New International Version (NIV)

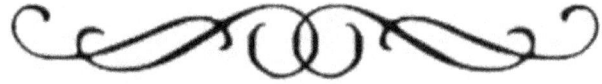

A woman who does not require validation is "a woman who knows who she is!"

MUSING

Life Can Sometimes Be a Blur

Truth lies in accepting where you are in the present moment of your life. Each day you decide to continue in forward movement, this is the day it will all come to full fruition. In my greatest times of fear, not knowing what the future would hold for me… I have learned how to laugh again. I laugh, I cry, and sometimes wonder why?

Yet I find myself pressing toward the mark. There is… "No Looking Back." I declare my life to be exceptionally full of love, joy, peace, happiness and contentment!

Judy F. Mojica

"No Looking Back"
by Damita Hadden

I am leaving this place now, letting go with all my fears, saying Good-bye to the memory I hold dear. I can finally breathe again.

It's a new day fair well past, as I close this chapter I set as free at last. I made up mind there's no turning back, the past is behind there's no turning back. I'm looking forward.

Not behind I've made a decision to give you my life and there's no looking back. Every step I take is new. I found courage to go on, though it's rough.

Sometimes I still have to be strong I may have to walk alone, But the one who lives inside me is always there to comfort and to Guide.

I can see the sun coming through the clouds, lift my head cause I'm alright now, I can shout about it. I can laugh about, I can talk about it.

How does this song resonate with you?

_____

_____

_____

_____

_____

_____

SELF-CARE
DEFYING ALL ODDS

Every waking moment I seek to better myself, I defy the odds. The only thing that can keep me from becoming all that I am created to be is me. I am therefore determined to go beyond all that I could ever think or imagine I could be.
Defying all odds!

FEAR

The greatest Challenge to overcome is
the one that lies within oneself!

YOUR JOURNEY

Never underestimate your ability to become all you are meant to be. With every failure, there is a success. This is your destiny…
this is your Journey!

MUSING

Sunday Evening Muse

Have you any boundaries, or are you simply living life carelessly and without caution? Every day of your life is filled with endless bouts of pleasures galore, that only satisfies for a brief moment in time.

Oh, to the contrary…they never seem satisfied. Once again, you are left feeling, lost, lonely, and empty.

It's like drinking from an empty cistern, head held back while tapping the bottom of a glass to see if there's more from where that came from. The more you seek to quench your thirst; every drop seems that much out of reach.

So, you keep going back for more. Failing to realize that what you're longing for you already have.

Sad but true, some haven't a clue of how blessed they are. Whether one seeks to be found or has found what one seeks.

You will never be complete until you're whole. Look for what you seek from within, learn to love yourself. By all means, learn to like yourself first and stop hurting those around you who just want to love you. Stop allowing others to hurt you.

Lastly, take pleasure in knowing He knows exactly what you need. Trust Him and never settle and never think you're missing out.

>   Remember...you're worth it!

LOVE

HOW DO I KNOW THIS IS LOVE?

Love falls within the confines of lust and like. It is quite evident that there is like, and the heightened sense of lust comes in like a flood and can sometimes subside over time.

After the honeymoon stage in the relationship has ended, this is when the true signs of love are felt by one or both partners.

Lastly, one might agree that true love is not found but experienced by two people who are willing to put in the **WORK** to make it all worthwhile in the end. Which, in turn, can lead to a lifetime of pure bliss!

We are often concerned about what we look like on the outside, rather than what we appear to reflect on the inside. Try building up your resistance to anything that causes you to not be the best you- you can be. Take the time out to love someone today by loving them unconditionally.... even if it pains you to do so. This is an exercise that is sure to get results!

But the Lord said to Samuel, "Do not consider his appearance or his height, for I have rejected him. The Lord does not look at the things people look at. People look at the outward appearance, but the Lord looks at the heart."

1 Samuel 16:7
New International Version (NIV)

THE ART OF LOVING

Stop telling people you love them if you're just going to treat them like the bottom of your shoe!

The "art" of loving unconditionally allows one the opportunity to enjoy immediate gratification without longing for it.

THE RISKS OF FINDING LOVE

Many are restricted and afflicted with the "Dis – Ease" of loving again, resulting in fear. Fear of failure. Fear of being let down or not living up to one's potential as a partner.

As we all are wanting and so desire to be loved and accepted by that someone special. This is a "risk" we all must decide upon. Are you willing to take the risk in finding love again?

The Real Question Here is...Is it Worth the Risk?

The love I show you will never be measured by the lack of love you've shown me.

Be in love with your life and take note that every waking moment is an opportunity to capture all that is meant to be. Never again say your life is over because things didn't go as expected or hoped for.

Just remember God always has a "ram in the bush" and is always on time. Now close your eyes...and take a deep breath, this is just the beginning of the next chapter in life!

Never expect that you'll be treated the way you treat others, and never take the blame when they reject your kindness.

Loving and being in love is not hard. Conversely, trying to love someone who does not love him or herself is what makes for an acrimonious relationship headed for disaster.

Ladies, make sure you take time to love yourself. You are worth every moment you decide to not answer the phone, change your name from "mommy" for a few hours, take yourself out for lunch, get that Mani-Pedi, draw a hot bath full of bubbles and pour your favorite drink. Don't forget that new book you have been waiting to delve into... (Smiling) and think about absolutely nothing...not to mention you are so deserving!

THE COLOR OF LOVE

The true fact about love and hate, neither sees color. The reflection is still the same, no matter how you look at it.

Nothing is more powerful...know this, when a man can keep a smile on your face and it's real, you'll never want to leave his side.

LOVING OTHERS

Think it not strange when you or the love you have to share with another is rejected. This is not a reflection of who you are, but rather that of one who has difficulty loving oneself.

At the end of the day...Owe no man or woman but to love them, even if from afar. Rest in knowing you have done your part.

Let no debt remain outstanding, except the continuing debt to love one another, for whoever loves others has fulfilled the law

Romans 13:8
New International Version (NIV)

TO LOVE AGAIN

The only way to love again is to allow oneself to feel beyond the pain of the past. You must not allow the pain of your past to dictate your future by holding on to things that you no longer have control over.

These life lessons are here for you to learn from them. Once you have mastered these lessons and have now come to an understanding of these "life lessons." You are now able to move forward to a full life of everlasting love.

I once thought I'd never love again. The thought of losing in the area of love again was unbearable. It was in my darkest days, where I encountered so many other women who were going through separation and divorce. Their stories were different, but the pain was just the same. We all were faced with change. As unfortunate as it may be with every season, there is change.

Whether it be in friendships, relationships with family members, a new love interest, relocation, a new home, career, car, job, weight loss or weight gain…it is all part of change, but there is one thing you must remember, where there is change there is newness of life and in this life is your opportunity to love again.

Musing on a Saturday Afternoon

A State of Contentment described by those who seek happiness in a crowd, at the next hottest event coming to town, or the gathering that will put them on the "map of popularity" is a true indication that those who are seeking a sense of belonging are "looking for love in all the wrong places."

Why does one seek to be known? Why does one seek to not only be heard but understood? Why does one feel the need to be accepted? Lastly, what exactly are we as humans lacking so desperately?

I believe the one thing we are lacking as the human race is contentment. The level of peace and contentment that can only come from the "giver of peace." A peace that surpasses all understanding. Why not seek to know the "one" who can give you life and that more abundantly and experience His goodness and mercy all the days of your life!

What level of commitment are you lacking?

_____

_____

_____

_____

PERFECT IMPERFECTIONS

Make no mistake it is in my "perfect imperfections" that makes the cut, color, and clarity of Carat-ter most profound. Make no mistake, I am still in the making of becoming His masterpiece. This is where the healing begins.

Name all of the things you see about yourself that are imperfections:

_____

_____

_____

NOW RELEASE THEM ALL AND BEGIN LIVING A LIFE OF WHOLENESS!

ABOUT THE AUTHOR

She is a prolific speaker of truth.

She understands the depth of pain of those who surround her daily. Beyond the accolades of educational institutions, awards or applause. There is a measure of wisdom, knowledge, and understanding that only comes from the greatest teacher on earth, better known as experience.

Judy, a true woman of faith, continuously walks out the plan and purpose for her life one day at a time.

As a divorced mother of two beautiful daughters, having studied at Light University, Mount Olive University and Rhema Bible College. Judy is a Bible Scholar, Educator, and Certified Professional Life Coach. She is also passionate with purpose and desires to help you reach the highest pinnacle of who you were created and meant to be in this lifetime.

When you spend time with Judy, you are the only one she sees as she is engaged so much, so you'll never have to wonder if you're being heard.

FROM THE HEART OF THE AUTHOR

If you desire to live a life of wholeness and understand how to go from point "A" to point "B" I believe I can show you how...not by words alone, but by the life, I now live.

Contact me today for your next conference, women's retreats, or allow me to become your professional life coach.

But wait...there's one thing you should know. It will cost you. Here's what I mean. For me to truly help you...you must be willing to bring all your broken pieces to allow God to put them back together again to create the masterpiece you were originally meant to be. Trust him to master your peace. Let me be clear. You are not a mistake. There comes a time in life we must all reach beyond our capacity to heal ourselves. Yet, the things we encounter in life whether self-inflicted or not…Life happens. I am a true believer that all things work together for the good of those who love, trust and are called according to his purpose. We all have an assignment to show up. So, let me help you be the best you can be. Remember it's not about me ~ I am here for you!

CONNECT WITH JUDY

Facebook: www.facebook.com/jfmojica1

Instagram: OutofBrokenness_

Website – www.bit.ly/OutofBrokenness

Email - MasterpieceCoaching1@gmail.com

Certified Professional Life Coaching also available for women of all ages. Specialized discipline for those who are divorced.

His Glory Creations Publishing, LLC is an International Christian Book Publishing Company, which provides publishing services for clients. They help launch and scale the creative works of new, aspiring and seasoned authors across the globe, through stories that are inspirational, empowering, life-changing or educational in nature, including fiction and non-fiction.

DESIRE TO KNOW MORE?

Contact Information:
CEO/Founder: Felicia C. Lucas
Website: www.hisglorycreationspublishing.com
Email: hgcpublishingllc@gmail.com
Phone: 919-679-1706

Judy F. Mojica